TinkerActive

EARLY SKILLS **WORKBOOKS**

Ages **3+**

Motor Control

written by **Enil Sidat**

educational consulting by **Casey Federico, MSEd**

illustrated by **Leo Trinidad**

odd dot

NEW YORK

120 Broadway
New York, NY 10271
OddDot.com

ISBN: 978-1-250-78437-7

WRITER Enil Sidat

ILLUSTRATOR Leo Trinidad

EDUCATIONAL CONSULTANT Casey Federico, MSEd

CHARACTER DESIGNER Anna-Maria Jung

DESIGNER Tim Hall

EDITOR Nathalie Le Du and Peter Mavrikis

Printed in China by Hung Hing Off-set Printing Co. Ltd., Heshan City, Guangdong Province

First edition, 2023

1 3 5 7 9 10 8 6 4 2

Meet the MotMots!

Amelia

Brian

Callie

Dimitri

Enid

Frank

Crayon Control

Welcome to Tinker Town's railyard!
Draw smoke coming from the train.

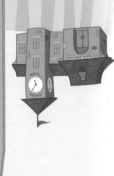

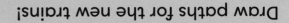

Draw paths for the new trains!

Frank spilled paint in the garage!
Draw the paint on the floor.

Enid, Amelia, and Dimitri are expecting a storm.
Draw the wind and rain.

Draw light from the lantern to show Brian the way.

Callie is loading wood onto the train.
Draw tree logs on the train car.

Brian and Amelia are cleaning the train.
Draw water spraying from the hose.

Dimitri is filling the truck.
Draw water pouring from the
water tower into the truck.

BE PROUD! STICKER

Enid and Amelia are shoveling coal into the firebox.
Draw flames to make the engine go!

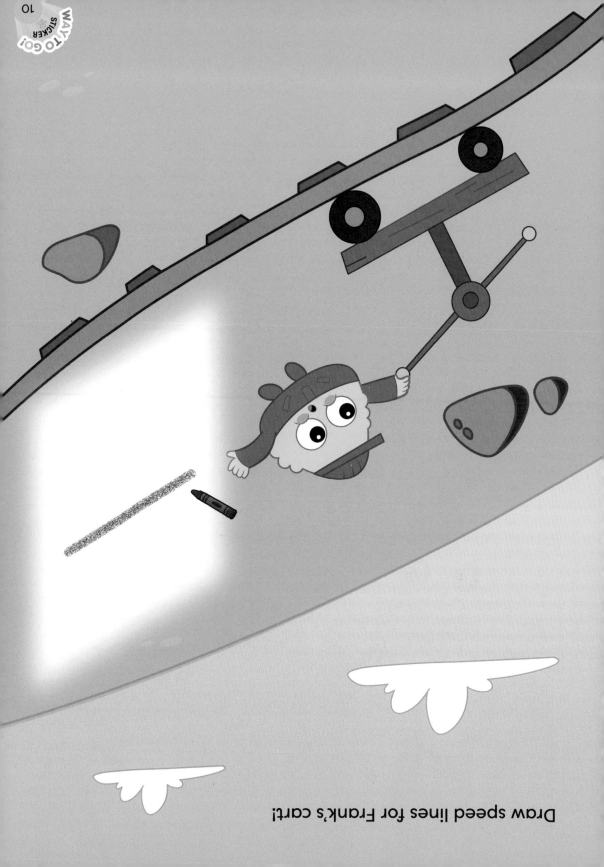

Draw speed lines for Frank's cart!

Draw dust and gravel flying away from Frank's hammer.

★ HEY, GROWN-UPS! ★
Scribbling in horizontal and vertical motions is the first step for drawing letters and numbers. Help your child practice scribbling in horizontal and vertical motions on the write-and-wipe game board by playing a game akin to Simon Says. Point your finger at one side of the board and say, "Draw this way, please!" Your child must scribble in the direction you point, but only when you say "please."

11

The MotMots are headed back to the railyard after a long day. Draw circular clouds in the sky.

EXCELLENT! STICKER

Let's TINKER!

Gather these tools and materials.

Tinker with your materials. **Roll** the crayons. **Rub** them across the paper. What do you notice about your crayons and paper? Can you make shapes with them, like a tree trunk or a car?

Crayons

Paper

Large poster board or recycled cardboard (optional)

Let's MAKE! A Tinker Town Train!

1. **Peel** the train sticker from page 128.

●●●▶

2. **Place** a crayon on the sticky side of the colored flap.

3. **Press** the rest of the sticker tape together. You've got a train!

★ HEY, GROWN-UPS! ★

You can find all the stickers at the end of this book. Peeling stickers is great practice for improving fine motor control. If your child has difficulty at first, peel up one corner and ask them to remove the sticker the rest of the way. Your child will gradually develop the skills to peel and place stickers on their own!

Let's **ENGINEER** a solution!

Amelia needs to make tracks for Dimitri's train, but she doesn't know where to start! How can Amelia plan where her tracks should go? **Draw** a long track that goes all over your paper or cardboard. Can you follow the path with your crayon train?

You're a TinkerActive CHAMPION!

You've earned an extra-special sticker. Peel it and place it anywhere you'd like on your poster.

Coloring with Crayons

Frank and Amelia love to ride their motorcycles.
Color their helmets.

★ HEY, GROWN-UPS!

We've intentionally created spaces with large buffers so you won't have to worry about your child coloring outside the lines. For now, your child is just getting comfortable with learning to fill in spaces. Encourage your child to color the white space and don't worry about perfection.

Color the headlights of the car
so Brian can drive at night.

Color the traffic light green so the cars *go, go, go.*

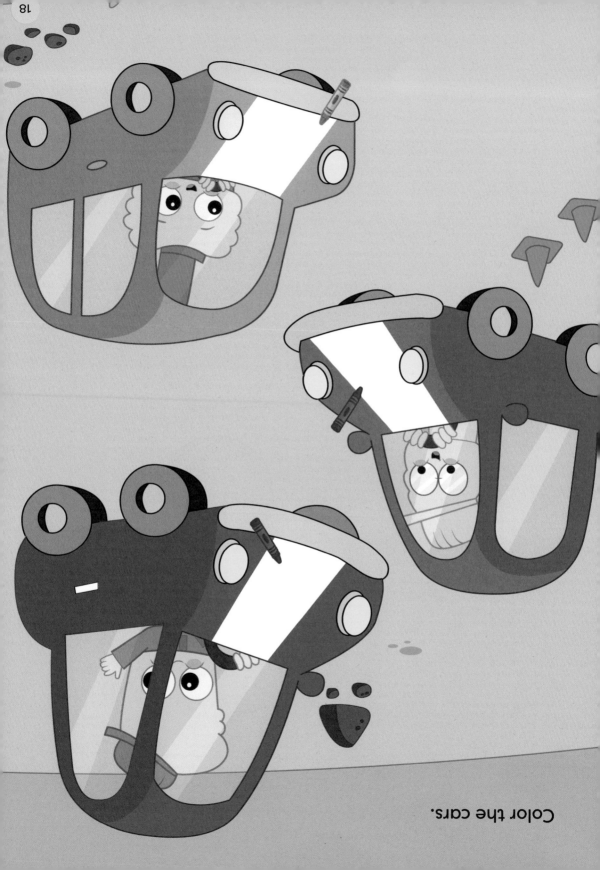

Color the cars.

Callie is making repairs! Color the potholes to fill in the road.

GOOD JOB!
STICKER

19

Color the fruits in the trees.

It's time for the Tinker Town Grand Prix! Color the car.

Amelia is going on a trip! Color Amelia's luggage.

Callie is bringing balloons to Enid's birthday party. Color the balloons.

GREAT WORK! STICKER

Enid is a daredevil, but she also loves safety! Color the cushions.

Amelia made direction signs for her street. Color the signs.

Frank is painting lane lines on the street! Color the lane lines so the cars know where to drive.

Color the dashboard buttons and steering wheel.

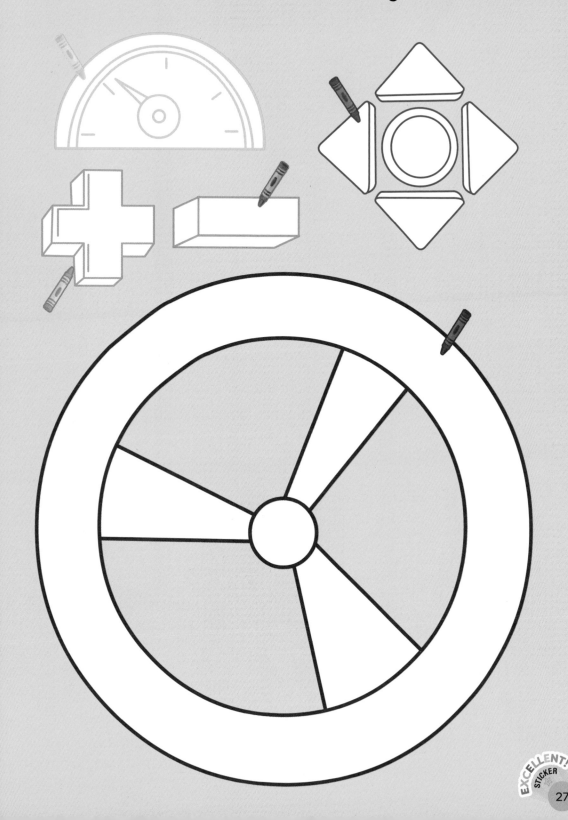

Color the Tinker Town
rainbow bridge.

Let's TINKER!

Gather these tools and materials.

Roll, spin, and toss your stones. Do your stones feel the same or different? Are some rougher and some smoother? What do the shapes of your stones remind you of?

4 or more small stones

Washable finger paints

Paint brush

Washable black marker (optional)

Let's MAKE!

Stone Cars!

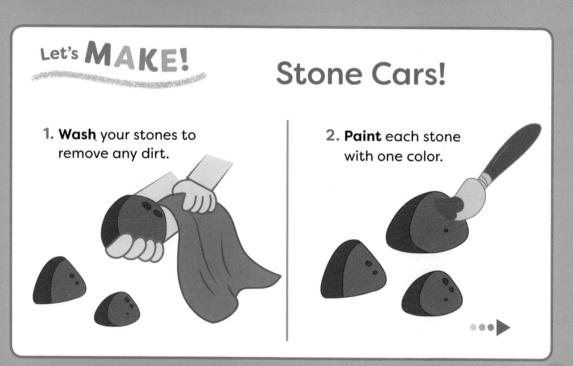

1. **Wash** your stones to remove any dirt.

2. **Paint** each stone with one color.

3. Let dry. Then add white windows using your fingertip as a stamp.

4. Let dry. Use black paint or marker to add details, like wheels, doors, and door handles.

Let's **ENGINEER** a solution!

The MotMots are having a stone car race! They want to **paint** their cars their favorite colors. But they only have red, blue, and yellow. How can they mix their paints to make more colors?

You're a TinkerActive CHAMPION!

Pencil Control

The MotMots are on the go! Draw paths for each MotMot to follow.

The MotMots need a break! Draw leaves to give them shade.

★ HEY, GROWN-UPS! ★

Early pencil control is simply your child scribbling with a pencil in a large space. Don't worry about their being neat or making realistic drawings. Instead, encourage your child to explore how the pencil draws and feels when they push softer or harder. It's also okay to keep using crayons if that's what motivates your child to continue practicing!

WELL DONE! STICKER

Draw a cloud of dust behind Amelia's dirt bike.

★ HEY, GROWN-UPS!

You may notice that your child uses a "fist grab" to hold their pencil instead of holding it between their thumb and fingers. You can show your child how you hold a pencil, but don't let correcting them stop you all from having fun coloring and scribbling. A correct grasp comes with lots of exposure to fun art activities.

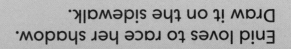

Enid loves to race her shadow.
Draw it on the sidewalk.

Draw water on
Frank's slide.

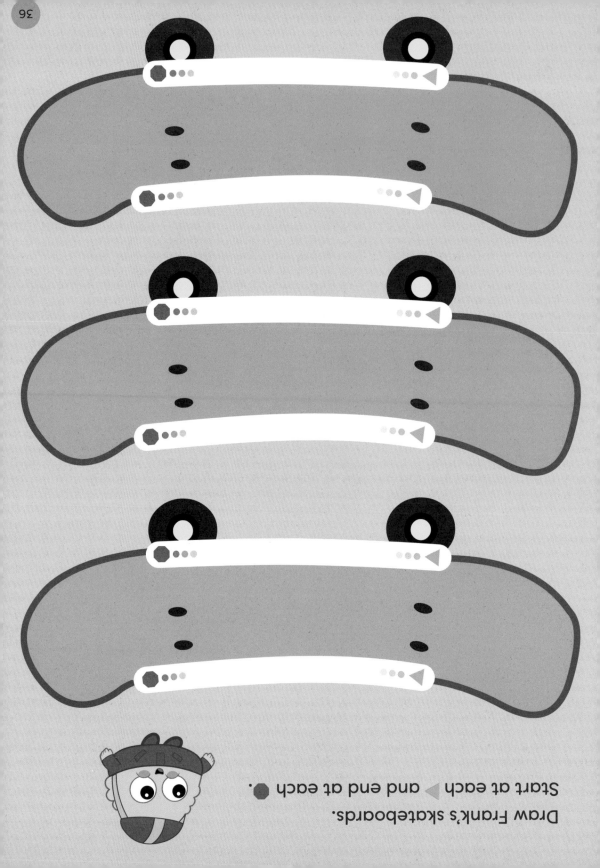

Draw Frank's skateboards.
Start at each ◀ and end at each ⬡.

Draw speed lines from Dimitri's scooter.

Brian and Callie are on their way!
Draw their paths. Start at each ▲
and end at each ⬤.

Draw streamers on each handlebar.

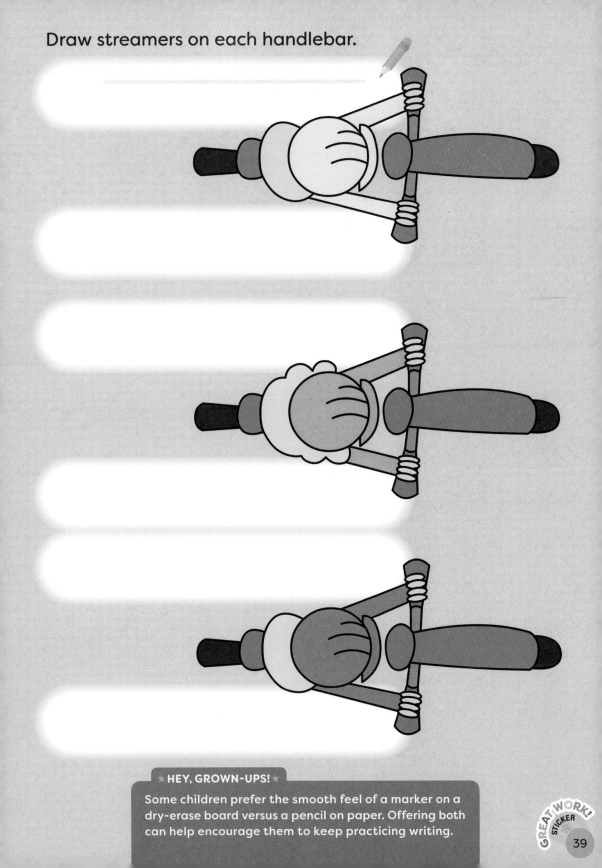

GREAT WORK! STICKER

The MotMots want to jump rope. Draw lines to make the ropes. Start at each ▲ and end at each ⬣.

Draw water spraying from the Tinker Town splash pad.

Amelia is trying to make her bike float away. Draw strings from the balloons to the handlebars. Start at each ▲ and end at each ⬣.

Draw leashes from Enid's hands to the dogs.

WAY TO GO! STICKER

The dogs in the neighborhood are taking Enid for a walk! Can you draw a leash from Enid's hands to each dog?

★ HEY, GROWN-UPS! ★
Games are a great way to practice drawing with your child. Try teaching them games like "dots and boxes" by using the write-and-wipe game board.

Gather these tools and materials.

Tinker with your materials. Is the eraser hard or soft? Is it flat and new or has it been used? Is the pencil point sharp or rounded? If it's sharp, how can you make it rounded?

Pencils (with erasers)

Washable ink pad or washable paint

Paper

Tape

Scissors
(with an adult's help)

★ HEY, GROWN-UPS! ★

This is a great opportunity to ask your child to think about all the ways they can hold a pencil to make different marks. Try holding the pencil straight up from the paper. Now hold it at a more horizontal angle. Does it make different types of marks?

Let's MAKE!   Stamp Art!

1. With the help of an adult, **cut** out the heart image.

2. **Tape** the picture to a piece of paper with tape loops or double-sided tape.

3. **Press** the pencil eraser into the ink pad and then stamp along the edges of the heart.

4. When you've filled the image, **remove** the cutout. You've made stamp art!

Let's ENGINEER a solution!

All the wheels of Brian's toys have gone missing. How can he replace the missing wheels? Can you find objects around your house that would make the right size stamps?

You're a TinkerActive CHAMPION!

Mazes with a Pencil

The MotMots are traveling all around town!
Write a line from Frank's  to the 📪.

Write a line from to the .

Write a line from Amelia's  back to .

★ HEY, GROWN-UPS! ★
Help your child navigate the maze with their finger before using the
pencil. It is okay if they go outside the path. Encouraging your child's
effort rather than their result is a great way to teach persistence.

49

Write a line from Amelia's  to the  .

Write a line from  to the .

Write a line from 🐱 back to his 🏍.

Write a line from Brian's  to the .

Write a line from  to the .

GREAT WORK! STICKER

Write a line from Enid's  to the .

BUNGLEBURG

Write a line from Enid's to the BUNGLEBURG.

Write a line from Callie's  to the .

★ HEY, GROWN-UPS! ★

If your child is enjoying the mazes, try using the write-and-wipe game board to create a maze together. Ask them how many turns they would want in the maze, how many dead-ends, and how many split paths. Let them describe as you draw the first few mazes. Then change roles.

MAIL

Write a line from the to the .

Write a line from  to the .

Write a line from the to the .

Let's TINKER!

Tinker with your materials. Can you roll the marble around the paper plate and keep it from falling?

Paper plates

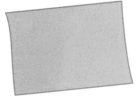

Construction paper

Tape

Marble

Scissors
(with an adult's help)

★ HEY, GROWN-UPS! ★

As your child plays with the materials, ask them about what they observe. If the marble keeps falling off the paper plate, ask how they can modify the plate to keep it on. (Hint: You can use plastic wrap to enclose the marble run.)

Let's MAKE!

Paper Plate Marble Run!

1. With the help of an adult, **cut** 3–4 strips of construction paper about the width of a thumb by the length of a hand.

● ● ● ▶

2. **Fold** a tab about the width of your thumb on each end of the strip.

3. **Tape** the tabs to the plate to create arches.

4. **Roll** the marble around to make it go through each archway.

Let's **ENGINEER** a solution!

Callie is delivering gifts to the MotMots in her neighborhood. How can she plan her route so she doesn't miss a MotMot? **Trace** a path on your paper plate so your marble goes through every archway. Then **test** it out with your marble. Can you draw longer and shorter routes with different color crayons?

You're a TinkerActive CHAMPION!

Brian loves riding the bus.
Write a line from
each  to its  .

WELL DONE! STICKER

Plan the bus routes with Brian.

Write a line from each  to its  .

Frank wants to keep the bus station clean. Trace the line from each piece of  to its .

Frank mops the floors.

Trace the line from each  to its .

Amelia is on her way!
Trace a line from

each  to its .

Amelia is driving passengers home. Trace a line from each  to its .

Callie helps people find their bus.

Trace the line from each MotMot to their  .

Callie delivers the bags.

Trace a line from each

MotMot to their .

Write a line from each to each MotMot.

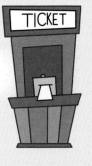

 Enid gathers all the tickets!

Write a line from each  to its  .

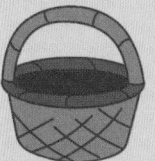

Dimitri puts new tires on the buses. Write a line from each  to its 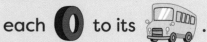.

Dimitri rolls the old tires away.

Write a line from each 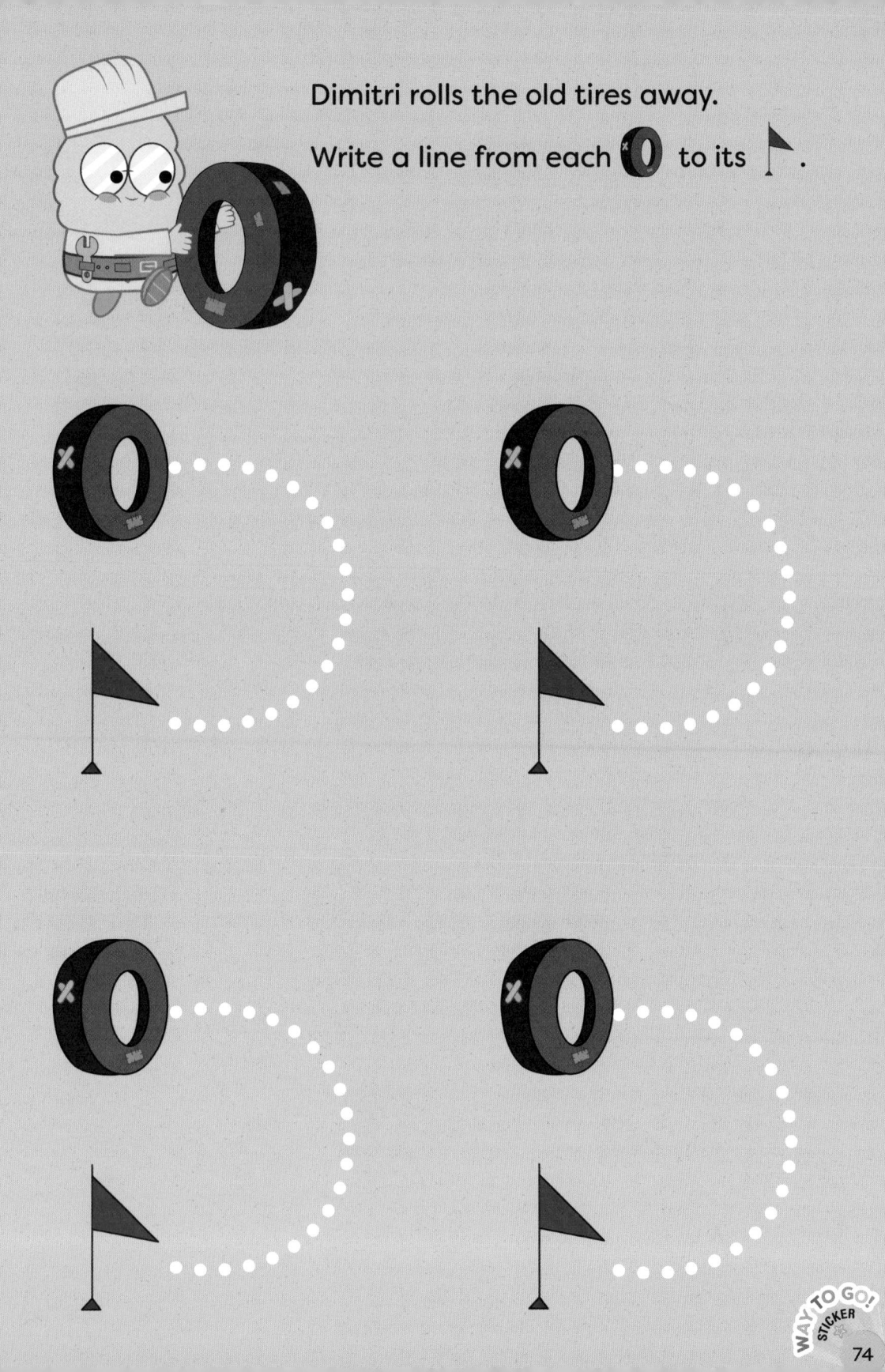 to its .

74

The bus takes the MotMots all around Tinker Town.

Write a line from the  to the .

The bus drives around the roundabout.

Trace the line from the 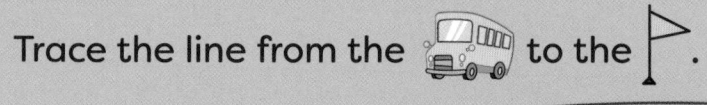 to the ⚑.

Let's TINKER!

Gather these tools and materials.

Tinker with your materials. Can you roll the bottle caps? Does the plate fold easily?

Paper plate

Bottle caps

Glue

Markers and/or crayons

Colored construction paper

Pencil

Scissors
(with an adult's help)

Let's MAKE! A Tinker Town Bus!

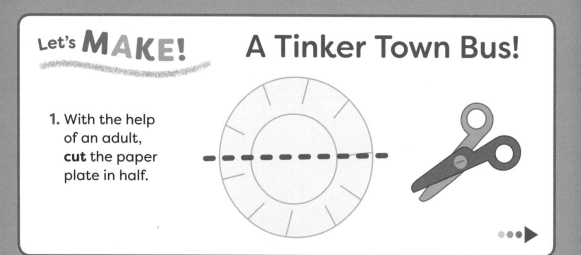

1. With the help of an adult, **cut** the paper plate in half.

●●● ▶

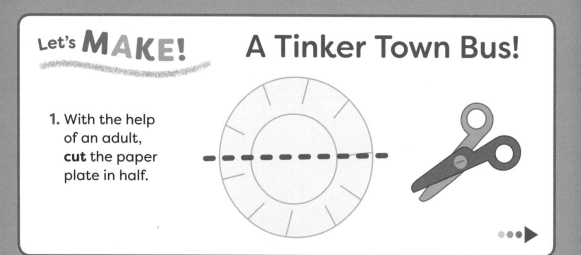

2. **Decorate** your bus. What color is it? Where are the windows? Who will be inside the windows? How can you show what you imagine?

3. **Glue** two bottle caps to your bus to make wheels.

★ HEY, GROWN-UPS! ★

This craft is designed to be open-ended to encourage your child to use their imagination and express themselves. You can even use the write-and-wipe game board to design a bus before gluing anything down.

Let's ENGINEER a solution!

Enid wants to ride the bus. But she needs help. How can she catch the driver's attention? **Think** about different ways to catch a person's attention. Loud sounds, big signs, and flashing lights might help. What can you build with your materials and objects from your home that could help Enid?

You're a TinkerActive CHAMPION!

Stickering

Here comes the trolley! Callie's ready to drive all around Tinker Town!

Sticker the trolley and MotMot onto the map.

★ HEY, GROWN-UPS! ★

Peeling stickers is great practice for improving fine motor control. Don't worry about the orientation of the stickers, or if they bubble or overlap as your child places them. The goal, at first, is for your child to master the simple act of applying the sticker to a sheet of paper. Watch as they progress quickly!

Sticker the MotMots onto the
subway platform.

TICKET

WELL DONE!
STICKER

Dimitri is looking for his tools.
Sticker the tools onto his tool belt.

Amelia is juggling!

Sticker the objects above Amelia.

Brian is checking the subway map.

Sticker the  onto the train tracks.

Sticker Frank and his alligator onto the subway seat.

★ HEY, GROWN-UPS! ★

Encourage your child to place the stickers in the space provided, but don't worry if the stickers are crooked or upside-down when compared to the background. Ask them about the characters and what they are doing. What does your child see? Where do they imagine the train going?

YOU DID IT!
STICKER

Sticker the  onto the tracks.

Enid is selling candy at the kiosk.

Sticker each  where the candy is displayed for sale.

Amelia plays music with her band.

Sticker the  and onto the drum set.

★ HEY, GROWN-UPS! ★

Instruct your child to hold the sticker above the page and turn it around until they think it's just right. Then have them place it. Say something like, "I really like how you think about where you want the sticker to go before you place it."

Dimitri changes the light bulbs on the trolley.

Sticker the  into their sockets.

Frank is inviting all of Tinker Town to celebrate friendship.
Help him sticker  and for his party.

Brian is naming the new trains.

Sticker the 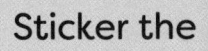 onto each train.

Everyone is going to Frank's party.

Sticker the  into their hands.

It's time for cake!

Sticker a  onto each empty plate.

EXCELLENT! STICKER

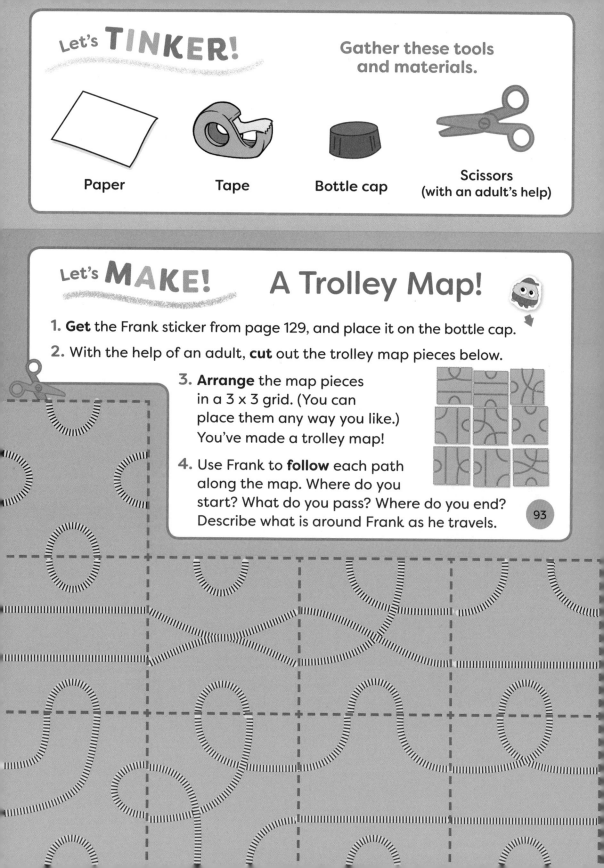

Let's TINKER!

Gather these tools and materials.

Paper

Tape

Bottle cap

Scissors
(with an adult's help)

Let's MAKE!   A Trolley Map!

1. **Get** the Frank sticker from page 129, and place it on the bottle cap.

2. With the help of an adult, **cut** out the trolley map pieces below.

3. **Arrange** the map pieces in a 3 x 3 grid. (You can place them any way you like.) You've made a trolley map!

4. Use Frank to **follow** each path along the map. Where do you start? What do you pass? Where do you end? Describe what is around Frank as he travels.

93

You're a TinkerActive CHAMP ON!

Let's **ENGINEER** a solution!

Frank is riding the trolley. Can you find the path that goes through the most tiles? Can you find the path that goes through the fewest tiles? Use your Frank token to **trace** the path. Try to **count** aloud the tiles you pass through.

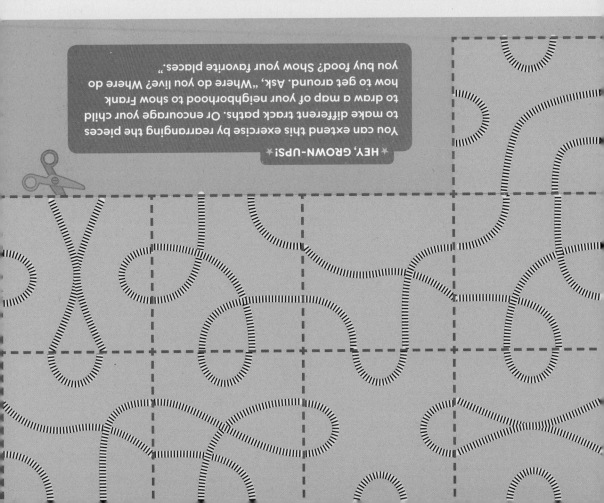

★ HEY, GROWN-UPS!

You can extend this exercise by rearranging the pieces to make different track paths. Or encourage your child to draw a map of your neighborhood to show Frank how to get around. Ask, "Where do you live? Where do you buy food? Show your favorite places."

Tearing Paper and Using Glue

Callie is arriving at Tinker Town's airport. Tear "clouds" out of the blue paper below. Then glue them to the sky.

Callie is labeling her luggage in case it gets lost. Tear "patches" out of the pink paper above. Then glue them to the luggage.

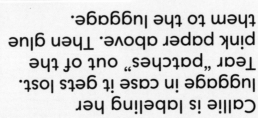

Frank needs his boarding ticket!

Tear the  out of the blue paper below.

Then glue it to Frank's hand.

ONE FARE

ONE FARE

Frank also wants a ticket on his alligator's tummy.

Tear the  out of the yellow paper above.

Then glue it to the alligator's tummy.

Amelia works in the hangar! Tear the wings out of the paper below. Then glue them to the plane.

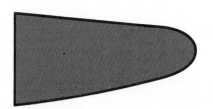

That was hard work! Amelia wants a drink of water. Tear the  out of the paper above. Then glue it in Amelia's hand so that the water will pour out.

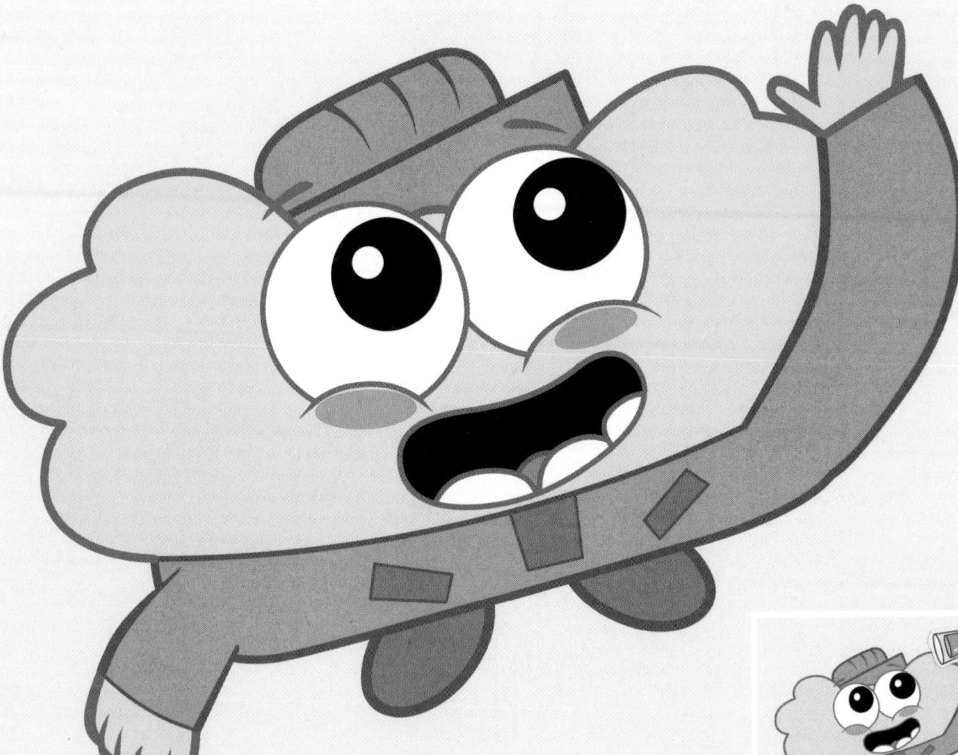

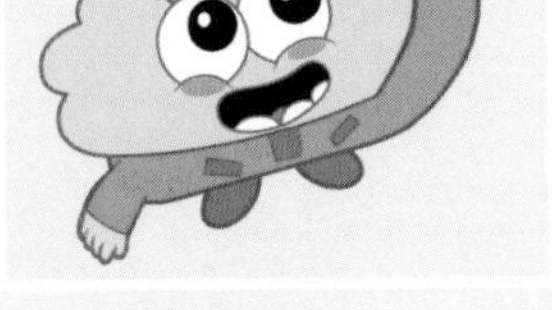

★ HEY, GROWN-UPS! ★
Using bottle glue is messier than using a glue stick, but it offers better practice for fine motor control and grip strength.

Dimitri is a pilot. Tear the  and  out of the paper below. Then glue them on Dimitri.

★ HEY, GROWN-UPS! ★

Ask your child, "Dimitri is imagining that he is a pilot! What do you imagine you could be?"

101

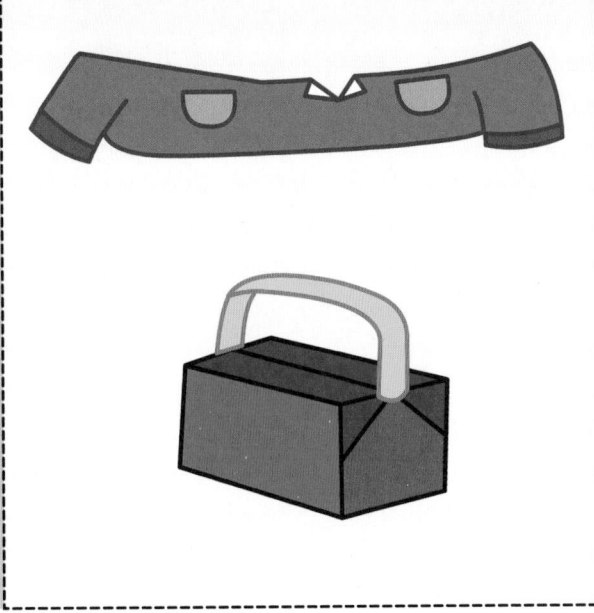

Amelia is a helicopter mechanic.

Tear the  and  out of the

paper above. Then glue them on Amelia.

Brian drives the shuttle! Tear the shuttle cars out of the paper below. Then glue them behind the cab.

Brian fills the food tray. Tear the  and  out of the paper above. Then glue them onto the tray.

Enid drives the baggage train. Tear the luggage out of the purple paper below. Then glue it on each baggage cart.

Enid uses a conveyor belt to get luggage onto the plane. Tear the bags out of the blue paper above. Then glue them onto the conveyor belt.

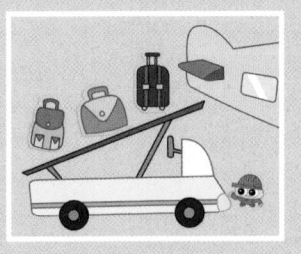

The MotMots are ready to fly.

Tear  and out of the blue paper below. Then glue them in their seats.

Frank waves to his friends on the ground. Tear the  and the two vehicles out of the blue paper above. Then glue them on the ground.

Let's **TINKER!**

Gather these tools and materials.

Experiment with your new materials! **Pour** some glue into a bowl. Does it flow like water, or is it thick? **Use** the craft sticks to stir. **Tear** some paper and dip it into the glue. What can you stick the paper to?

Wooden clothespins

Craft sticks

Markers

Glue

Bowl

Paper

Let's **MAKE!**

Clothespin Airplanes!

1. **Decorate** three craft sticks and a clothespin with your markers.

●●●▶

2. **Glue** two craft sticks to the top and bottom of the front end of the clothespin.

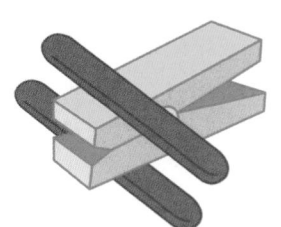

3. With the help of an adult, **break** or **cut** about a thumb's length off each end of a craft stick.

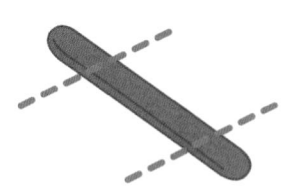

4. **Glue** the center of the broken craft stick to the top of the back end of the clothespin.

5. **Glue** one of the broken-off pieces to the tail of the plane, standing straight up. Let it dry, then fly your plane!

★ HEY, GROWN-UPS! ★
As your child applies the glue to the craft sticks, help them by holding the pieces together until the glue sets.

Let's ENGINEER a solution!

Amelia wants to enter the Tinker Town Flying Machine Competition, but she doesn't have a design. Can you help her design a flying machine?

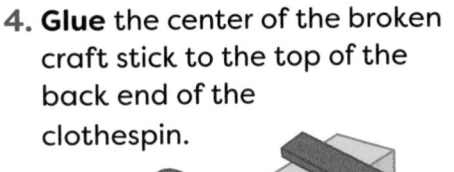

You're a TinkerActive CHAMPION!

Folding Paper

Frank is waiting for his ship to arrive. Fold upward along the ·········.

★ HEY, GROWN-UPS! ★

Fold blue dotted lines ▪▪▪▪▪▪▪ **upward**, which will bring the sides facing you together.

Fold orange dashed lines ▬ ▬ ▬ ▬ **downward**, which will bring the sides facing away from you together.

★ HEY, GROWN-UPS! ★

Folding paper is a fine motor skill that takes a lot of practice—but it's worth the time! Simple origami develops fine motor control, spatial reasoning, geometry, hand-eye coordination, and more!

Fold downward along the ------- .

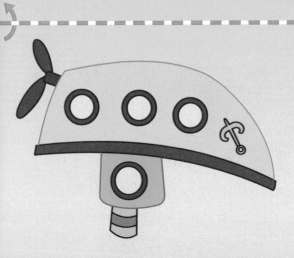

Help Brian catch a fish.
Fold upward along the ·········.

Fold downward along the

The MotMots had a great day at the harbor.
Fold upward along the ········.

★ HEY, GROWN-UPS! ★

Encourage your child as they try to coordinate both hands to work together. Ask them, "Can you push down on the paper slowly to control where it creases?"

Dimitri drives the water ferry.
Fold upward along the · · · · · · · · ·.

Fold downward
along the ---------- .

Callie is snorkeling, but the fish are shy! Pull this page out of the book. Then fold downward along the ------.

★ **HEY, GROWN-UPS!** ★
After your child makes the fold, show them how to create a crease by dragging a finger over the edge of the paper.

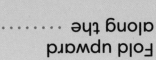

Fold upward
along the

Amelia is looking for a whale.
Pull this page out of the book. Then fold downward
along the – – – – – and upward along the ⋯⋯⋯.

Enid is looking for pearls.
Pull this page out. Then fold
downward along the - - - - - - -
and upward along the ·······.

Fold downward along the ⋯⋯

Fold upward along the ⋯⋯

Gather these tools and materials.

Roll your paper. **Tear** it and fold it, too. **Fold** or roll pieces of paper together. Do any of your actions leave marks? How does the paper change shape?

A few pieces of paper

Glue

Crayons

Let's **MAKE!**

A Paper Boat!

1. **Take** one sheet of paper, hold it vertically, and fold the top half down.

2. **Make** one diagonal fold from the top-left corner to the center.

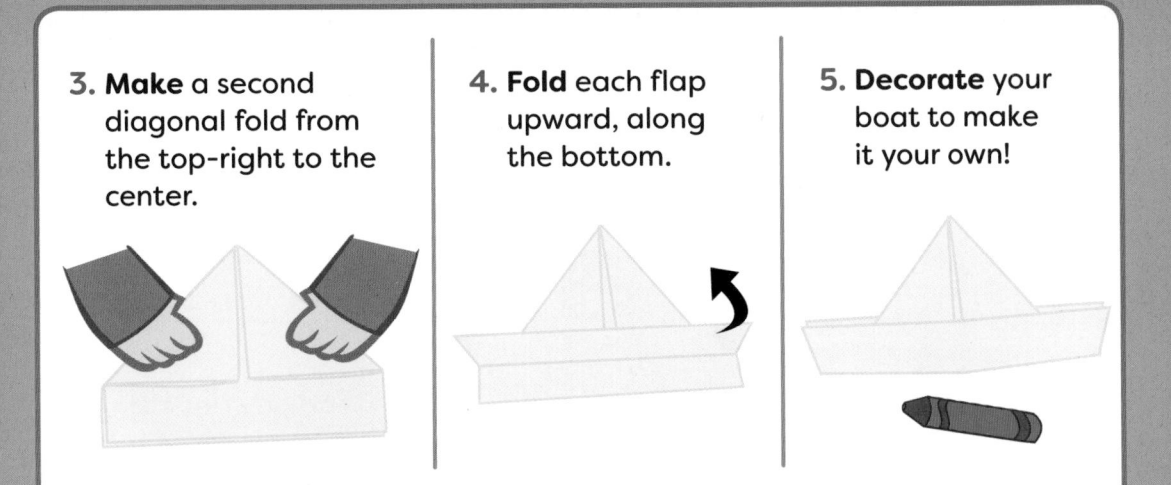

3. Make a second diagonal fold from the top-right to the center.

4. Fold each flap upward, along the bottom.

5. Decorate your boat to make it your own!

★ HEY, GROWN-UPS! ★

This final project is just a bit more challenging than the others. Take it slowly and help your child with each step. This is a great opportunity for your child to practice focus and perseverance. And it's a perfect moment to praise your child for their concentration and progress!

Let's **ENGINEER** a solution!

Frank and Enid want their paper cutouts to go on the boat. But the waves are high, and the boat is rocking up and down. Can you think of a way their cutouts can stay on the boat?

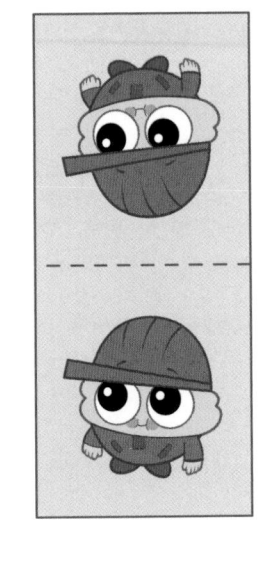

You're a TinkerActive CHAMPION!

Exercise Stickers Page 13:

Page 79:

Page 80:

Page 81:

Page 82:

Page 83:

Page 84:

Page 85: